Andrew Graves has been avc
preferring instead to spend
poetry. As no one has tried t
continue with this aimless lif
the end of the Tenner was rel
Jean 'Binta' Breeze as 'A breath of fresh air. ____
his Saboteur Award Shortlisted show God Save The Teen –
essentially a story about growing up and getting it wrong. He is
currently writing this biography. Don't let the third person thing
fool you, it's definitely me / him.

God Save the Teen

Andrew Graves

Burning Eye

This edition published by Burning Eye Books 2017

www.burningeye.co.uk
@burningeyebooks

Burning Eye Books
15 West Hill, Portishead, BS20 6LG

ISBN 978-1-911570-02-8

'Ceremony', 'Something Brave and Ridiculous', 'Johnny', 'Saturday Night and Sunday Mourning', 'Soldiers', 'The Blue Bench', 'Not All Monsters Come in Kits' and 'Alan Moore' were all previously published in *Citizen Kaned* (Crystal Clear Creators).

CONTENTS

Car Crash Smiles

Watch Like No One's Dancing

God Save the Teen

Silk-Lined Floozies with Tailored Scars

CAR CRASH SMILES

Some days I'd like to have all the optimists shot for being cowards.

Rab C Nesbitt

Junk

The charity shop window
displays an ancient copy
of Sinatra's *Songs for Swingin' Lovers*;
a 50p label gags the crooner's lips.

The guy staring in
neither swings nor loves,
hampered by damp sleeping bag,
his songs are morning spare change pleas
repeated, replayed.
His dance an awkward two-step
avoiding bus lane soakings.

He gives a Monday comeback concert
for an audience
of rain.

No adoration, just reflection,
kinship in a silenced voice,
Old Blue Eyes strikes an awkward
bargain.

They agree to be forgotten,
battered, alone,

scratched by different needles,

sold off
way too cheap.

Lip Service

The Goose Fair had been and gone.
I was just a kid. I'd got into this bad habit
of licking my lips.
All the time.
Tongue whipping back and forth
through missing teeth, a pale
and scruffy lizard boy.

By November they'd got bad.
So dry and cracked they became infected.
My mouth swelled, a raw weeping wound,
a strawberry scar spreading beneath my nose.
An eight-year-old Joker, crying, not laughing.

She attended, carrying out threats
of TCP administration, pain sending me
into spasms and tantrums,
bubbling away into smileless, sulking
Sunday teatimes.

After a while they got better.
Broken sores replaced with
Friday evening chip shop grins.

To ward off any further occurrences,
she armed me with my own
lip balm. A tiny tin pot bought from Boots
the chemist years ago, selected from
her cabinet of medicines, make-up and
women's things.

It held my tongue, comforted me,
I slathered it on during those unkind months.

Eventually the summer came with its
Robin Hood adventures

and crappy homemade arrows, fired into
the distance, aimed at school holidays
and fragile futures of fun.

Then, when I was eleven, she left,
taking the cabinet and
its secrets of soothing lotions
with her.

I saw her once a fortnight,
both of us pretending
that things were good,
things were the same.

Knowing the bond was as broken as those
cracked winter lips.

Visits became phone calls,
rare and tired little testimonies, birthdays,
bank holidays and
cautious Christmas
promises I knew
would stay
unwrapped.

Now, on those October
nights of Goose Fair rattle,

I find my hands dug deep into
pockets of the past,
cold fingers searching for
that tiny tin pot
of soothing balm,

finding only lint.

Ceremony

Via pylon mascots and manky roads,
homes without names and lost postcodes,

from the reek of skunk and Asda beans
stride the Burger King and his Bedsit Queen.

A romance born at the corner shop,
two star-crossed lovers in tracksuit tops,

a Valentine written on an old scratch card,
stolen flowers from a posh house yard.

Their love spins round like kebab-house meat,
wrapped in moonlight and dying streets,

till it's consummated in the underpass
among wet chip-wrappers and broken glass.
They emerge embarrassed, wasted and sweaty
to shower in the headlights and raindrop confetti.

Something Brave and Ridiculous

For Brian Clough

Something brave and ridiculous jack-knifes up the pitch,
hard, thin, socialist, genius streak of piss,
cold eyes, soccer-blind, destroys the green and white,
puts the ball, and any hint of doubt, in the corner out of sight.
Clad in ivory, blood-red trails,
cracked bones, goals and Holy Grails
where careers crunch and fail in the rain-black mouth
where two posts, a keeper and God can take you out.

Something brave and ridiculous growls, dug-out to pitch,
green jumper animal, mouthy son of a bitch,
colder eyes, still lost in *that* face
screaming sermons of words: *You're a bloody disgrace,*
and the League knows and Europe knows and En-ger-land calls
but two-finger handshakes say it's all a load of balls.
Wherever greatness was, the whisky broke it down,
a pock-marked retirement is Big 'Ead's lost crown.

Something brave and ridiculous stands near to Slab Square,
tarnished bronze, hands aloft, silent victory prayer,
barked orders to ragged pigeons echo City Ground dreams,
shopping centre tackles and long-retired teams,
the spirit of '77 fully realised above
turns cartwheels on a sixpence forged in fire and love…
And the penalty box lies empty, bar the stud-marked torn sods
where the referee calls time on this game of men and gods.

Irony Man

The bloke on the bus warns
that the planet Earth is in imminent danger,
that toothaches are caused
by the CIA,
that cats are government agents,
that terrorists are planning to microwave the moon,
that the Prime Minister is a lizard person
and the Queen has evil powers

but, far from being grateful,

repelled by that shell of
untouched armour,

the world he so desperately wants to save
rolls its eyes, yawns

and moves to another seat.

Burglar

She came in through
little Sammy's window.

His dad took a poker
to the back of her head.

The cops could make
no sense of the dead intruder's

flimsy pink get-up or the bag
of baby teeth

spilled upon the floor.

Ray

We listen for the ghost
of the Dring-Drang Man,
guitar case bank of
coppered-up tunes,
denim and beret
crash with beaming smile,
framed in Neil Young's
harvest moon.

Dylan's heartbreaks
and Cat Stevens hits,
requests for
rusted angels, lost,
shopping bag rustle
of damp applause
finds a summer of love
in a Mansfield frost.

Weeding out dances
in the old town square
in the taproom of the Market pub,
where the old guys wept
to dreadlock licks
and Guinness soaked
up the buskers' club.

When a day's betrayal
was strummed away

in finger-brittle, smoking songs,

loved-less lovers
and an unplayed riff,
reminders where
he once belonged.

On the high street
where the Woolworths was,
with its legacy of cheap-arse
Primark clones,
we look for the shadow of
the Dring-Drang Man,
in the spectre of pennies
that remain unthrown.

Coasting

Chip forks are makeshift
spears of destiny,
skewering the fat of the seaside world,
as blind waves carve out landscaped tales
into marbled hills under awkward skies.

Drawn uninvited to crashing voids
via beachy heatwave buckets of fun,
we buy our tickets to ways which turn
on nature's rickety fairground ride.

We sit by bunkers smoothed by years,
hear sing-along siren, ice cream wars,
watch squads of gulls drop spattered bombs
on bodies bleeding factor 10.

So we make our toasts in flat warm beer,
take our vows in the knicker-slipped dunes,
carry the present of rolling tides,
cross thresholds in sea-damp

shoes of sand.

Johnny

He takes on the crowd in a pincer attack,
the Country Boy bleeds and he bleeds black.

Wears his coat like dark brushed skin,
whip-smart, piece of art, vampire-thin.

Tongue that cuts like a razor blade,
nuclear bomb in wrap-around shades,

with a line in violence and winkle-pickers,
powder, pills and Southern liquor.

Brylcreem quiff and bootlace ties –
no reason to die or apologise.

No reason for reasons, just truth in his eyes,
shit-kicker grin with heart in the skies.

Slick and unashamed, dangerous to love,
devil with a six-string sent from above.
A ruinous and beautiful hymn about to crash,
the gallows gospel poet: *Hello, I'm Johnny Cash.*

The Working Dead

Wakeless drivers
window shop
at railings stocked
with roadside blooms,
a special offer
rush hour deal
on poster kids
with car crash smiles,

on grieving potholed
grey wet skin,

each tyre a dead-lipped
goodbye kiss.

WATCH LIKE NO ONE'S DANCING

Things just seemed to go wrong too many times.

Tony Hancock

Saturday Night and Sunday Mourning

I dreamed I was with Arthur Seaton last night,
watched him swagger down streets cast in black and white
in Saturday suit, all hard-bastard pretty,
wondering what became of his Sunday morning city.
Showing two fingers at speeding cars,
kicking in windows of Yates's Wine Bar,
searching for factories that just weren't there,
hosed away fast as vomit in the square.

Demolished and built on like the back-to-backs,
he wondered why history'd given him the sack.
How was he so young, yet broken and old?
Burned by today, chilled by fifties cold.

Between fights and ale and fat arse slander,
no good times left, just propaganda,
I screamed, 'Alan Sillitoe's dead' – he looked at me, then spat.

'Alan Sillitoe?' he said. 'Who the fuck's that?'

Flea Market Forces

It will come again tomorrow

with its broken biscuits, dodgy trainers

and a bloke called Steve doing
three lighters for a quid.

None of it is worth having
but no one round here
can afford

not to buy it.

Soldiers

They kiss by the memorial,
his lips cold
as railings at her back,

poppies and used confetti
waltzing awkward through headstones,
names that mean nothing
and years less.

Unlike the Great War
                    it'll be over by Christmas.

The Blue Bench

Where the war will come to smoke,
take off its uniform,
rest in ill-fitting dressing gown
and standard-issue pyjamas.

Where it will remove its helmet,
show its true face
and whisper old warnings on
newly constructed lips.

Where it will kiss lost sweethearts
and show us how to
count our blessings on
blistered stubs of fingers.

During the First World War, Queen Mary's Hospital, Sidcup, was one of the few places in the world to pioneer brand new plastic surgery techniques. Patients were encouraged to take in fresh air during treatments; however, those soldiers whose injuries were horrific enough to be deemed visually 'shocking' were asked to sit at specially designated blue benches, away from the gaze of other patients.

Iceland

We tramp from plane
through glacial gusts,
wrapped in sulphured
mystic threats,
seek staves tattooed on
tax-free ale,
in airport
Viking-plundered shops.

We ride like ghosts
on skeletal ships,
text sagas on
our mobile phones
that capture ice sheet
mountain tops,
lonely trails
and sleeping seals.

We cool our drinks
in April snow,
cleanse in desolate
hot tub finds,
chase stray dogs
through a magic den
of dolphin skulls
and tourist
spells

We make a feast
of baked fish soup
in a shack of shadow
by moon-skimmed lake,
while the glow of witches
on history's pyres
lights our way
on
last
chilled
miles.

Darth Santa

Star Wars is Christmas.

Expensive, at least three of them have been rubbish
and everyone hopes the next one
will be the one they
had when they
were six.

Cheers

It was a place full of
those who'd never tasted the truth
and those who were choking on it.

No satnav required, just take
every wrong turn, you'd get there soon
enough.

No last orders,
just constant reminders.

Its doors remaining open,
like a badly healing wound.

Austerity Soliloquy

I watch the bitter playground
of some distant prince
whose slings and arrows
offer suffering
and outrageous misfortunes,

in a red top slanging match,
spewing out a sea of trouble
that flows into the gennels
of the undiscovered counties,

forming pangs of the despised
who huddle in the food bank queues,

cast as characters in life's waiting list,
a poorly written production
penned by villains forgiven,
knighthoods where their
souls once were.

Backyard Battles

Washing line shirts
twist in upturned
dance of surrender,
and I willingly join them
caught in the crosshairs
of a rifle-lens spider web.

Then, a fleet of sycamore helicopters
make their unplanned attack
and I am casual casualty.

Part naked body
stretches beneath
the promise of a miracle
and blackbird mourning melodies
sung from sky-broke lines.

A kettle whistle bugle blows
and the war is won.

Dumping Ground

She might tell me
at the supermarket
where trees
are strained with
carrier bags,
window shopping
for a better view.

She could break my heart
in the bowling alley
where the burgers taste
of greasy death
and families
strike up nights of
hope, that clatter
down the polished
lanes.

The final kiss might
linger where
gardens bloom
with white good rust
and mangled prams
and Christmas trees
and busted
moss-green paddling pools.

But instead she takes
me by the hand,
last words
saved for better streets.

Edinburgh

The city yawns,
a rallying victor
in fringe incursions,
its blurred eye blinks once,
redder, wiser
than its London version.

Out of Season

You're the mist that clothes the snaking bay,
a cold snap bitter promise sewn,
tailoring the cliff-bound castle,
cockleshell shivering spectral chic,
an autumn style for housing stock,
bric-a-brac shops and back-to-backs.

You're the actors on the promenade,
forgotten winter, seaside roles,
smudges that perform their work
as unheard, unwatched mystery plays
where rainy curtains batter down
on narrative's worn-out limestone stage.

You are the sea, the universe,
a choppy forever of white crashed prayers,
saline psalms of eternal spray
preaching to graffiti clouds
that canopy the fisherman
on aching, moon-cast Jesus shifts.

You're the distant cars from north and south,
approaching lovers on dusk-draped roads,
the unavoidable fogged affair
that's driven through the heartbroke night,
the hoped-for kiss that's narrowly missed,

the headlight bleeding nothingness.

God Save the Teen

Since 2012, some 600 UK youth centres have been shut, 3,650 youth staff have lost their jobs, and 139,000 youth places have been axed. As an ex-youth worker and as a writer who has worked consistently with young people for years, I find these statistics shocking, so I decided to write a show which, at least in part, aimed to highlight some of these issues and the possible consequences of not having a well-funded youth service. It was directed by the ultra-talented Rob Gee and is about the most personal thing I've ever written. I'm extremely proud of it and I'm still touring with it now. Presented here is a written version of the show.

God Save the Teen

I'm going to come clean.

With a heart beating, old soul retreating
ricochet into yesterday.
A monologue writ by the old pit tip,
a council house of love
and unwashed dishes,
the broken-up kisses of an
ex-Mr and Mrs.

Where roses were bled
and violence was true
and life ganged up to
beat us black and blue.

It's about the generation gap
and all that crap and it's a
little sentimental but I'll take that wrap.
It's about the missing spaces
and turned-away faces,
messed-up school yards and long-forgotten
greeting cards.
It's about a time of a funny Valentine.

I'm going to come clean.

Please, God save the teen...

1981

Ronald Reagan, the Yorkshire Ripper, Bobby Sands, Buck's Fizz...

I'm being dragged backwards over the seats of a bus filled with psychopaths. My nose is bleeding, my body's covered in various cuts and bruises and Kerry King keeps punching me in the balls.

Kerry King is huge and hairy and a complete bastard.

His nickname is King Kong. Unfortunately, unlike his namesake, in this story he doesn't end up falling from the Empire State Building having been riddled with bullets from enemy planes.

He just keeps punching me in the balls.

The driver is trying to pretend that World War Three isn't happening in the back of his bus. He simply pulls his cap down, puts his foot to the pedal and tries to get his vehicle to its final destination in one piece.

I, on the other hand, am trying to get my body to its final destination in one piece, with considerably less success.

Somehow I end up at the back of the bus. My arse lands in a pool of Fanta; at least I hope to God it's Fanta. I try to stand up but fall over again. Someone has tied my shoelaces together.

It's at this point that my eyes meet with those of Sally Jenkinson. She's easily the best-looking girl in the school, all golden-tongued hair and too much blusher, like a junior Cheryl Baker. Our joint gaze seems to go on for all eternity and momentarily I'm lost in her loveliness until those oh, so luscious, oh, so kissable lips say...

'HE'S PISSED HIMSELF! HE'S PISSED HIMSELF!'

This earns me another punch in the balls from Kerry King – who's nothing if not consistent.

Then I notice the straps on my new Star Wars *backpack, the most precious thing in the world to me, have broken off, caused by being dragged backwards over the seats.*

In that second I feel an overwhelming surge of anger. I want to unleash the Force upon them like Obi-Wan Kenobi, want to crush the throat of Kerry King, Darth Vader style. I want to lop off the arm of the driver with a trusty lightsabre and I want to crash the Millennium Falcon *into the big fat gob of Sally Jenkinson.*

I don't do any of those things. In fact I do the one thing you shouldn't do in that situation, when you're eleven.

I start to cry.

Eventually we arrive at our destination and the driver, with all the empathy of an SS officer in Bethnal Green, pushes me off the bus.

For a while I sit on the low-slung wall which runs around the bottom of the estate. I try to undo my shoelaces and stop crying. I achieve neither. It's a warm, sunny day but suddenly I'm enveloped by a cold, dark shadow. I look up expecting another kicking from Kerry King; instead I find myself staring into the face of my father.

I have no idea why he's there, he never meets me off the bus, he barely even speaks to me. He simply looks down, sees my face caked in blood and snot, my shoelaces tied together, the suspicious wet patch on my trousers, shakes his head, then says:

'Your mam's left home.'

Dad

I was raised in a small mining community, soon to be ex-mining community, called Sutton-in-Ashfield. It wasn't everyone's cup of tea, I'll grant you. Some said it was a shithole, but we didn't care; at least it was our shithole.

The estate I lived on wasn't too bad – a far cry from the demonised estates of today's modern media – but for all that I never really felt as though I fitted in and I certainly didn't have many friends.

My dad didn't help matters. He wasn't exactly a glowing example of paternal care.

His idea of a fun family day out consisted of buying me a stale Cornish pasty from the pit canteen before taking me to the cattle market to watch frightened cows go off to slaughter.

Saturday mornings were always him crouching over the betting pages, Grandstand on the telly, beer gut spilling out of his egg-stained vest, the remains of the week's pit dust still clinging to his eyes making him look like a lardy Alice Cooper.

Living with him could be difficult.

For a start he had a seriously bad flatulence problem.

He also liked to cough up phlegm, sometimes so violently that his false teeth would fly out, and his favourite food in the world was a cold Brussels sprout sandwich, smothered in Daddies brown sauce.

Which more than likely accounted for the flatulence problem.

He would also sleepwalk on regular occasions, and this wouldn't have been too bad were it not for the fact that he always insisted on going to bed in the nude.

It could get very, very embarrassing.

Mr Smith

As well as having to put up with my dad, I also really hated school. And the thing I hated the most about school was PE.

PE teachers are like poets. Everyone knows that they're doing a pointless, made-up job – everyone, that is, except them.

Mr Smith, our PE teacher, was no exception; he was less a man and more of a lobotomised pit bull in a faded rugby league shirt.

He used to turn up to school on a massive vintage motorbike, which I'm convinced he only bought because it saved him the job of having to develop an actual personality, and he had this loud monotone growl and called everybody lad, regardless of their gender. More disturbingly, though, he insisted on wearing these green tracksuit bottoms that were just a little bit too tight for a man who spent the majority of his working life hanging around children.

It was all kinds of wrong.

Mr Smith, who, worryingly, only lived two streets away from me, would assert his fairly limited powers by humiliating people like me in as many ways as possible. For instance, I would often find myself doing cross-country in the freezing cold rain, wearing only a vest and pants.

If I were lucky, it would be my own vest and pants.

And whenever we had to practice rugby tackles, he would always pair me up with Kerry King AKA King Kong, knowing full well he'd use it as an excuse to damage me in as many ways as possible.

But one day Mr Smith outdid himself.

The day after my mum left, the humiliations of the bus incident still buzzed in my head. Subsequently I arrived at school late and in my rush, I forgot to pack the standard issue white plimsolls I knew I needed for PE. I tried to explain the situation to Mr Smith, tried to appeal to his better nature but *quickly realised he didn't have one. He just went ballistic. He punished not just me but the whole class by making us all run round the outdoor tennis courts in our bare feet.*

This wouldn't have been so bad, but the tennis courts were pretty much unused except at night by the local winos. As a result the courts were littered with shards of broken glass.

Miraculously most kids, not all, got around unscathed, but not me. I slipped and stepped straight onto a broken piece of Newcastle Brown bottle. Fortunately I didn't need stitches but it did bleed quite heavily, leaving me with a pronounced limp for about a week and a half, which my dad completely failed to notice, being either too drunk or too wrapped up in himself.

The thing that Mr Smith hadn't counted on, though, was that if you collectively punished a whole group of children, you also simultaneously collectively pissed off a slightly bigger group of parents. So it was no complete surprise to us when he turned up to work one day with a split lip and the remains of a black eye.

It seems that Mr Smith, he of the very wrong trousers, had finally picked on the wrong kid.

1996

The Dunblane massacre, Monica Lewinski, Clinton, cigar, girl power...

It never occurs to me that Selena isn't her real name.

I'm a youth worker, have been for a year or so. The youth centre I work in is old, crumbling and falling apart at the seams, and Selena, or so it's agreed by most of the kids that attend there, is the coolest thing in it.

She only ever wears black. Black with black, married with a hint of dark black. She isn't just a goth, she's a goth's goth, the gothest of the goths, she's gother than Dracula's pillowcase, gother than Death's underpants, she's goth squared.

She doesn't so much walk as float, a pale-skinned sixteen-year-old ghost with an attitude. She smokes cigarettes like Lauren Bacall and wears expensive-looking shades that hide carefully made-up eyes. She talks about Jack Kerouac and Jim Morrison and paints stories about her beloved nightclub Rock City.

What really adds to her mystique is that she only ever comes to the youth club once a week and only for an hour. After that she disappears into the night like a black velvet Cinderella.

She never leaves a glass slipper behind, but one day she does leave her bag.

It's a vintage-style thing, black obviously, the sort you might see in an old American film. The thing is we have no way of contacting her, so we just leave it behind the counter on the off chance that she pops in.

A week goes by, two weeks, three weeks. No Selena.

Some of the older youth workers get a bit concerned and it's put to me as the youngest member of the team to find out where she lives, take the bag as an excuse to see if she's okay.

To be honest, I don't really see what the fuss is about. I just assume that she's got bored of the youth club and run off to join The Cure or something.

I manage to prise her address from a kid called Kenny. He's a gormless-looking lad who has a serious crush on Selena. So much so, in fact, that he actually followed her home one night, fully intending to ask her out on a date, sweep her off her feet. But he chickened out at the last minute. He ended up hiding behind a wall, watched her walk inside and close the door and that was that. Her feet remained unswept and Kenny's romantic night out turned into a long walk home with a cold bag of chips.

I must admit I'm really curious about the kind of house she lives in. I know it's on the posh estate somewhere but I'm expecting some sort of Tim Burton-esque Gothic mansion, replete with gargoyles, Alien Sex Fiend blasting out through the black ornate carved doors.

It's nothing like that. It's just an ordinary semi.

Less Hammer House of Horror, *more* Homes Under the Hammer.

I mean, the front garden is slightly shabbier than the rest on the street and the obligatory Volvo on the drive has a suspicious-looking dent, but other than that it fits in perfectly with the suburban aesthetic.

I knock on the door and wait.

Eventually it opens and I'm immediately hit by the strong smell of disinfectant and recent sick.

A girl stands before me. She's wearing crappy old jeans, worn-out slippers and her faded top is covered in various food stains and God knows what.

I do a mental double take.

It's Selena.

The black crimped hair is scraped back into a practical ponytail, the make-up is gone and her outfit is more Sue Ryder than Siouxsie and the Banshees, but it's definitely Selena. She looks back, not so much surprised, more resigned, relieved even.

I can see past her into the living room. A gaunt-looking man is slumped in an armchair. An overflowing ashtray at his feet is flanked by a dozen or so empty cans of Special Brew. He lollops awkwardly to one side, his eyes in different orbits. He calls out, 'Maggie... Maggie.'

Selena turns around then, and says, 'I'm coming, Dad.'

Like I say, it never occurs to me that Selena is not her real name...

Selena

So, Selena, show us
your black lace dance,
a fishnet lie,
worn on Maggie's last chance,

a finger to made-up
gothic lips,
a daddy's girl rehearsed
in a shadow script,
a graveyard of empties
and off-licence bills,
into avenues of whisky
and a dad's broken will.

No Sisters of Mercy
in this convent of pain,
where velvet won't mix
with the dried vomit stains,
a dark web performance
into private hell,
a staged noir concert's
promise not to tell.

So, Selena, show us
your black lace dance,
a fishnet lie, worn on
Maggie's last chance...

I secretly hope that one day Maggie will make an appearance at the youth centre.

But she never does.

1986

Chernobyl, Libya, hand of God, Bon Jovi, hair…

Some girls these days look forward to leaving school with a prom. Back then, some girls I knew looked forward to leaving school with a pram.

I looked forward to leaving with nothing. No qualifications whatsoever.

My dad didn't seem to mind. He'd always seen exams as something posh people did to hide the fact they couldn't do something more useful – like arm wrestling.

My mum showed slightly more concern, but she was shacked up with her fancy man by then and I didn't want to get involved.

In retrospect it's a wonder my parents managed to stay together for fifteen minutes, let alone fifteen years. They were less an accident waiting to happen, more an accident rudely pushing its way to the front of the queue.

And I knew from personal experience that my dad was not an easy man to live with.

He'd been smoking since the age of nine, drank at least eight pints of bitter every night and devoured no healthy food whatsoever. Annoyingly, this only seemed to make him stronger. In short, he was like some sort of working-class Godzilla. I began to believe he couldn't be killed by conventional weapons.

And he was, or so I thought, about as romantic as a knackered old pit sock.

But this didn't stop him from putting it about a bit.

After the divorce, he went into what can only be described as his stud phase. What was really disturbing, though, was that he was actually quite successful.

I had to watch in abject horror as my dad, this car crash of a man, with false teeth and pot belly, made his way through the whole gamut of Sutton's womenfolk in about two and a half weeks flat, like a coal dust Casanova.

I on the other hand was sixteen, at the prime of my life, and the closest I'd come to a sexual encounter was when my hand accidentally brushed across the leg of a pensioner when I was reaching for a copy of **Kerrang!** *in the local newsagent's.*

He didn't half give me a funny look.

Things calmed down a bit after that, but then my dad was made redundant from the pit and as bad as that was, and it was bad, I think a part of him was relieved because he'd always really hated working in the mine. But it did put a lot more pressure on me to find some sort of work, any kind of work. As the cartoon character Top Cat once said, the grim spectre of employment was looming.

The dole office finally caught up with me and forced me onto a YTS.

YTS officially stood for Youth Training Scheme, but to the thousands of unscrupulous employers that had signed up for the project purely so that they could legally exploit kids for cheap labour, YTS became short for something else: 'You're Totally Stupid'.

I was made to go and work in the local Fine Fare; it's still there now actually, only now it's been converted into an Asda. I don't know about you but I seem to spend a lot of my adult life wandering around various branches of Asda. I've learned to see it as less of a shopping experience and more essential training for the inevitable zombie apocalypse. But back then it was Fine Fare, and for five days a week I was paid the princely sum of £27.50. Which when you think about it, in today's money, works out about... fuck all.

I really didn't get it. It was really tedious. Shelf stacking just wasn't my thing. So I went back to the dole office, and I asked them, no, I begged them to find me something, anything other than shelf stacking. Well, they looked at me a little bit snottily, like I was some sort of working-class upstart, and asked me what it was I thought I could do that would be so much better than shelf stacking, given the number of qualifications that I clearly didn't have.

To be honest, this kind of threw me, so I muttered something about wanting to work with animals one day.

Well, they sent me back to shelf stacking with a bit of a flea in my ear, but they did say that if anything came up they'd let me know. I didn't really hold out much hope though, just figured I'd be stuck shelf stacking for the rest of my life.

But just two days later I was transferred from shelf stacking into...

...the butchery department. Be careful what you wish for.

You see, the problem was that I was sixteen and obsessed with a band called The Doors. So a supermarket would never be interesting enough, would never be exotic enough and would certainly never be rock 'n' roll enough. Or would it...?

Unexpected Idol in the Bagging Area

You see, there ought to be a supermarket called *Jim* Morrison's.
Located on the corner of *Moonlight Drive* and *Love Street*,
a *Roadhouse Blues* for the *Break on Throughs*,
it would only sell whisky, fags and LSD.

Its café would be a *Soul Kitchen*,
where a *Light My Fire* burned up juju spells
in a leather-clad trip of tribalistic retail frenzy
into doors of perception, a two-for-one reduction
on an acid trance, death's last-minute sale,
where everything must go.

Shopping trollies pulled by nameless
Backdoor Men would be fashioned
from old Parisian bathtubs and
the tannoy would play *Riders on the Storm*
on a twenty-four-hour loop.

And instead of getting a basket
you retrieved a face from the ancient gallery
and walked on down the aisle,
to a place where mothers and sons
would come together and…

No golden ticket deals, just golden copulations,
LA Women lost in tabards of dreams,
shelf-stacking shamans saying *Touch Me Touch Me Touch Me*,
a *Soft Parade* promise made by the dented tins.

And when you paid for your goods,
a strangely familiar shop assistant,
the one who makes you crazy,
would pin a wild-eyed stare on you,
screaming, '*You are the lizard king, you can do anything!*'
And when the music was over
you would stagger out into oblivion,

finding yourself at the back of the queue
with your only friend,
singing this is
The End.

…Then I suffered the final indignity when I was moved into the warehouse, where my primary responsibility was stacking packets of toilet roll.

I decided to do something much more positive with my life.

I decided to get the sack.

It wasn't hard, actually. I had a warehouse full of expensive merchandise, a forklift truck and a very, very bored me.

You do the maths.

And it worked, and I was free.

My dad, though, who lavished much more attention on the carrots in his allotment than he did on me, didn't really see it that way. 'You've right boggered that one up,' he said, with all the warmth and charm of Genghis Khan after discovering he'd run out of pile cream.

I had to admit I was ready for him this time. I simply looked up into his jowelled unshaven face and said, 'Don't you worry, Dad. I'm going to be – a rock 'n' roll star.'

1999

Kosovo, the Millennium bug, Columbine, crap *Star Wars* film...

Somehow, somewhere Romeo and Juliet clash with the council estate and out of the wreckage crawl Sarah and Paul, their arms around each other, two fingers in the air, defiant.

Because life doesn't so much throw things at them as launch a nuclear attack, a hundred thousand megatonnes of bills, poverty, circumstance and more bills.

Barely out of childhood themselves, they have a kiddy on the way, and no proper home, unless you count their freezing cold flat, no carpet on the floors and mushrooms on the ceiling. Less a place you try to live in, more one you try not to die in. No friends or family, just a creepy landlord, who only ever calls round when he thinks Paul's not in.

All they want is some warmth and a cup of tea, and that's why they come to the youth centre. Usually they're happy with their own company. They huddle together, Sarah rolling fags for Paul, Paul gently rubbing her eight-month-old bulge.

But one day they let me in on their inner sanctum and they tell me about that time when they first met on that cold New Year's Eve...

Sarah and Paul

In a freezing fog there
is a low-slung kiss,
leopard skin wrapped
around a bone-sharp frame,

an embrace of mist
slopping tongues of spit
in a love as skinny
as a benefit claim.

A bent-double lust
against a rusting swing,
streetlamp roles
cast by God's own night,

phone text souls
merged with rain sludge park
in a digital version
of *Wuthering Heights*.

In a shivering rush
to fumbling depths,
fingers pull
on ladders of skin,

hot breath trails
into Christmas lights
while midnight chimes
court the council bins.

It's a dog-end scene,
frosted year's last gasp,
a hangover birthing

a broken time,

the deadbeat dregs

cling to cracked dry lips,

unmouthing the words to Auld Lang Syne.

1987

Thatcher, hurricanes, riots, Rick Astley...

I was the singer in a rock 'n' roll band called Whiplash Mascara. I modelled myself upon Johnny Rotten, Alice Cooper and Iggy Pop – but when you had all the charisma of a wet tea towel and the face of Rodney Trotter, it wasn't easy.

For the first gig, I wore one of my grandma's old blouses, make-up and an oversized crucifix. I thought this would make me look avant-garde. The problem was I had no idea what 'avant-garde' meant. Neither, as it happens, did the ex-miners who'd turned up to the gig thinking Whiplash Mascara was a female strip act.

How we got out of there alive, I'll never know.

But we did and after loads of hard work, determination, practice, practice and more practice, we became... barely any less shit than when we started.

Of course, my dad offered me no encouragement whatsoever. On his hate list, I think pop stars fell somewhere between politicians and child-murderers.

To be honest, though, I think my dad's anti-pop stance may have been a bit of an act. Because I once caught him dancing to 'YMCA' by the Village People.

My dad, the slightly homophobic borderline racist, dancing to a multi-cultural anthem about gay lifestyle – it was terrifying, like finding out that Hannibal Lecter was actually a peace-loving vegan.

It was around this time, though, that I got my second ever Valentine's card.

For the purposes of this story I'm going to say that the person who sent the card was called Madonna. Because, to be honest, I've always secretly fancied the real one, and it's my show, so I'll do what I like.

Now, Madonna became my first proper girlfriend. She was pretty, and she was kind, and she had this beautiful blonde hair that always smelled of angels – and I, well, I had absolutely no idea what to do with her.

It was like giving an iPad to a pensioner. They might look pleased but inside they're a maelstrom of confusion and resentment.

But it was special and I think I enjoyed being confused and I think she did too. Eventually, inevitably, we fell in love, till one night our thoughts turned to more physical concerns…

Naked

A balmy summer night,
alone in the living room,
Dad in bed,
lights out.

The TV jabbered to itself,
the moon poked through
a small kink
in the polyester curtains,

for a horny sixteen-year-old
with a crooked nose
and limited imagination
it didn't get much more
romantic than that.

Our bodies entwined
on an old sofa that smelled
vaguely of dog.

We swapped spearmint-flavoured kisses,
lost and found each other,
fumbled in the dark,
two inexperienced teens
about to embark

on the world's oldest sin.

Like my girlfriend's pop star namesake once said,

I was like a virgin – but not for much longer.

This was the night, this was really going to be the night when...

It was just a shape in the corner of my eye at first, a blurred, pink shape that shuffled towards me slowly. But as my eyes got used to the darkness I suddenly realised that it was...

Oh God, oh God, oh God...

That's when Madonna saw it too and that's when she started screaming, a bloodcurdling scream that wouldn't stop.

That's because coming out of the gloom, like a horrifying, half-cut phantom, was my sleepwalking father... COMPLETELY NAKED.

He lolloped closer, ever closer, until he was so close that —

Madonna stopped screaming.

This was replaced by a silent round-mouthed grimace, the sort you might make if you'd swallowed some of your own sick – or possibly someone else's.

That's because my father's testicles, his unveiled testicles were dangling perilously close to her head, like a pair of cold Brussels sprouts, almost touching that beautiful blonde hair that always smelled of angels.

Somehow I managed to frogmarch my unconscious father back to his bedroom, whilst Madonna got dressed.

But as I walked her to the bus stop, I knew something had been lost. With all the dignity we could muster, we kissed goodnight, but I knew I was really kissing goodbye to that beautiful blonde hair that always smelled of angels.

1992

John Major, Yugoslavia, Maastricht, new Dracula, Deeply Dippy…

My dad and me had never really got on but it was at that stage that we started to really, really not get on.

Everything he did seemed to get on my nerves. Everything I did seemed to disappoint him more and more.

It was like an invisible barrier had fallen between us, both of us on opposite sides, both of us desperately trying to think of something not to say.

Eventually there was nothing to say. The shouting stopped. The arguments stopped. Everything stopped. So I started packing.

I gathered together what I had, which wasn't much, few records and clothes, and threw them in a box that I used to keep things in when I was a kid, and that was that. I moved into a derelict house with a tattooist, a thief and junkie.

It was pretty grim. I never even unpacked properly, just lived out of that stupid box I'd taken from Dad's house.

I got a job in a record shop. It wasn't a good experience.

I started drinking heavily. I started turning up to work drunk, started to openly badmouth the company and on several occasions I fell asleep in the staff toilets.

I got the sack.

This time, not on purpose.

The thing is I was so out of it, I couldn't even figure out why they'd fired me.

There was trouble back at the derelict house too. The tattooist had taken to hanging mutilated baby dolls up in our front room window. The police were called but they were never fully forgiven for not arresting us on the spot.

You see, the neighbours thought we were monsters. In fact the closest we came to that was when we watched horror films on the old black-and-white telly we had.

We had no central heating so we'd wrap ourselves up in army surplus sleeping bags and eat Tesco Value brand baked beans.

Which caused a lot of flatulence.

The flatulence reminded me of my dad.

I started to miss him, and then I knew what I needed to do.

I did LSD, mushrooms, ecstasy, skunk, anything I could lay my hands on.

Anything but go and see him. I just had too much pride.

I think it's safe to say that the years between 1992 and 1994 were a bit of a blur and, in the words of Oasis, my life was beginning to Slide Away.

2001

George W Bush, twin towers, the war on terror, paedophiles, *Pop Idol*...

Joe seems to come out of nowhere and brings most of it with him.

He's older than the usual tracksuit and trainers lot. The Youth Project works with sixteen- to twenty-five-year-olds and Joe's definitely pushing the higher end. He takes most of the insults slung at him in his stride but in teenage terms he's the social equivalent of a skid mark.

He seems to be able to linger in dark corners even where there are no dark corners. He also has this look, a kind of haunted, resigned-to-a-life-of-drudgery look, which tells you that he has either a dead mother mummified in a cellar somewhere or, worse, a live one who still buys his clothes for him.

Aside from the odd wheezy cough and faint whiff of unwashed trousers, I hardly notice Joe's there at all.

One day, though, something happens. Some new kids drift in from the old estate, lads mostly, too young for the pub, too daft for sex.

Ego tells me they've come because of the fantastic reputation the youth club has; my head, though, tells me they've come for the cheap chocolate bars and free pool.

Amongst them are a couple of punks.

It's nice to see a flash of tartan and black leather, against the sea-blue striped Adidas and cheap shiny Kappa.

They're not the most seasoned of punks, it has to be said; one of them has lurid green hair, making him look like a spotty teenage Joker, whilst the other still has the price tag sticking out of his bondage trousers.

Joe seems to take an interest in them too.

They settle into the opposite corner and crank up The Clash's greatest hits on the oversized ghetto blaster they've dragged in with them.

This seems to agitate Joe; he begins rocking back and forth, wringing his hands.

Then 'London Calling' starts playing. That's when it happens. As though under some CIA mind control Joe immediately stands up, marches quickly over and asks them to turn the music off. Green Hair does what any seventeen-year-old would in that situation: the complete opposite, he turns the music up. Joe just stands there, like his brain is trying to compute some impossible equation or like he's reliving some half-remembered story.

Green Hair starts laughing and Bondage Trousers joins in.

I don't even see it happen. No one does. It's too fast. Joe's fist rams straight into the soft pudgy face of Green Hair, who reels back aimlessly. Blood is already streaming from his nose. Then Joe lays into Bondage Trousers, pushing him over a nearby chair. As he goes down, Joe sticks a boot in.

By this time, I'm racing across the room. I get there just in time, manage to grab the ghetto blaster from Joe's hands, just as he's about to bring it crashing down on Green Hair's head.

I chuck it to one side; it lands with a crack on the floor, causing the CD inside to skip endlessly on a single lyric. Another youth worker calls an ambulance, whilst I drag Joe into a different room, the mangled Clash song following us down the corridor... London's calling... London's calling... London's calling... London's call—

As the heavy fire door blanks the music out, Joe seems to calm a little. I sit him down in the nearest chair but it's like he's not there anymore, he's disappeared somewhere, his eyes lost in another time.

I know I have to call the police, I know there's going to be trouble, I know there's going to be an investigation.

Above all I need to know why. Joe snaps out of it then and for a second I think he's going to turn his fists on me.

Instead he just looks at me with those strange hollow eyes...

Billy Boy and Joe

This is the story of Billy Boy and Joe,
a junkie *Jackanory* from a short time ago,
of borstal botherers who did mind the bollocks,
beer-fuelled estate kids, punk-rockaholics.

How they beamed down like a sci-fi scene,
two discount spacemen, no arse in their jeans,
a secret for the universe, a gospel tattooed,
unrighteous brothers, a brew half-stewed.

A gormless duo on a toxic trip,
one guitar between them they'd found in a skip,
three chords and the truth and a rubbish song,
a set list that came in at five seconds long.

They were just remnants blind with rock 'n' roll eyes,
stooges of love kissing crucifix skies,
Sid Vicious chancers and record thieves,
their escape routes formed by the bands on their sleeves.

Then the city was calling, that cruel little circus,
the *roll up, roll up* for the desperate and surplus,
they were searching for the future and their own rebirth
and all they found was the shittest show on earth.

They faced long nights on streets of old souls,
a cold comfort Christmas with the last of their dole.
No glamour or groupies or backstage pass,
just doorways, bus stops, then a thing called smack.

And Joe just watched as his best mate cooked,
saw his eyes go out to lunch and come back fucked,
watched the kid he'd grown up with, the daft lad from school,
sink into a gutter lined with needles and drool.

Saw the methadone promises get shot in the head
with Sex Pistol dawns and things never said,
in the anarchy of being, the heartache pinpricks,
where a brown town crippled those teenage kicks.

And Billy Boy whispered his last war cry
and he pogoed his way to that gig in the sky,
no bands on his sleeves, no music in that face,
just a track-marked map to a lonely, lonely place.

Joe's wake-up call was a body bag,
best mate stubbed out like twos-up on a fag.
Someone called an ambulance, someone called the law
and Joe didn't want to be a punk no more.

It's a story told from the point of no aim,
a kerbstone banality of unplayed games,
an undone narrative where the heroes don't win,
an apology of rust under fragile skin,

of old paths clogged with brick dust bags,
the heroin chic of a casket dragged
through a lovin' spoonful, artery squeal,
the breakdown decision, laced chemical meal

and they'd beamed down like a sci-fi scene,
two discount spacemen, no arse in their jeans,
a secret for the universe, a gospel tattooed,
unrighteous brothers, a brew half-stewed.

Beer-fuelled estate kids, punk-rockaholics,
borstal botherers who did mind the bollocks,
a junkie *Jackanory* from a short time ago,

that was the story of Billy Boy and Joe.

1995

Blur, Oasis, Tarantino, *Toy Story*...

Things were bad, I seemed to have no friends, I hadn't seen my dad for two and a half years and I had what I discovered later to be some sort of nervous breakdown.

It wasn't pretty and, as we've already established, neither was I.

Despite this, I managed to meet and fall in love with the person I would eventually marry.

Her hair was neither blonde nor smelled of angels – but she was ace.

She came from a really close-knit family and so she had a hard time understanding the way that my own family completely failed to function.

She pressured me into going to see my dad. I was resistant at first, even resented her for suggesting it.

But I went.

When I was on the bus I started to feel angry. I started to list all these things I wanted to say to him. I wanted to ask him why we'd never really talked. Why he felt he couldn't show any emotion towards me other than a begrudging pat on the shoulder, if he was half pissed, and why he seemed to blame me for my mum running off like that.

Each item on the list burned brighter and brighter, hotter and hotter, and as I got close to the house, I found I couldn't even breathe.

But as I walked up the path he came out to greet me.

It had only been a few years since I'd seen him but it could have been ten. He looked older, greyer.

But as our eyes met his face did something weird. I think it was smiling.

We had a cup of tea and we talked about stuff, nothing important, nothing heavy, and the list I was carrying in my head seemed to get lost somewhere.

It didn't seem to matter anymore.

What did any of it matter anymore? So what if he was gruff, aloof, a bit of an emotional vacuum? What had his worst crime been, really? To stick by me when everything went tits up, and how did I repay him? I buggered off at the nearest possible opportunity.

I know he wasn't perfect, but who was?

Things got better after that. I even went back into education. I began to feel a lot better about myself, I had found some self-respect, and much to my surprise I began to actually look forward to seeing my dad.

And all this would have been brilliant had my dad not done something completely out of character.

He died.

The man who I was convinced could not be killed by conventional weapons was killed by the most conventional weapon of all – a stupid bloody heart attack.

Two weeks after the funeral, my girlfriend asked me to move in with her.

I finally got to unpack that stupid box I'd been carrying around with me since I'd left my dad's. I took out the old clothes I no longer wore, the records and a few tapes, and underneath everything was a battered old pink envelope.

It was something I'd not seen for years.

If pushed, most blokes will tell you that their first ever Valentine's card was actually from their mum, but I knew mine was from my dad.

Even at eight years old I'd worked it out. I recognised his scrawled semi-literate lettering. Not only that, he had tried to write the phrase 'From an admirer' three times but he kept spelling the word 'admirer' wrong, so in the end he'd crossed everything out and simply wrote 'From a lass'.

And it was then, sitting there in my late twenties, with the daft card in my hand, that I began to see just how much that emotionally bankrupt, gruff ex-miner had actually cared.

A few days later I ran into Kerry King. To my surprise, he didn't try and ram my head into the nearest toilet. Instead he offered to buy me a pint. I was distrustful at first, but like all ex-school bullies he had eventually turned into something smaller and less significant.

We got to talking about school, him managing to carefully skirt around all those times he'd made my life a complete misery, but eventually we got on to Mr Smith, the PE teacher. We both laughed about the time when he'd turned up to school that day with a split lip and black eye. And I said, 'Did we ever find out who'd done that to him?'

Kerry just looked back at me blankly and said, 'You mean your dad never told you?'

Yeah, turns out, after all those years, I was that wrong kid.

I got involved with the youth service, first as a volunteer, then as a paid employee. But they didn't just give me a job; like my dad before me, they gave me a chance.

Years later I decided to try my dad's recipe for a cold Brussels sprout sandwich, smothered in Daddies brown sauce.

You know what? It tasted really...

...fucking awful

So, God save the teen,
I've just come clean
with a heart beating, old soul retreating
ricochet into yesterdays,
a monologue writ by the old pit tip,
a council house of love and unwashed dishes,
the broken-up kisses of an ex-Mr and Mrs.

Where roses were bled
and violence was true

and life ganged up to beat us black and blue...

GOD SAVE THE TEEN
Dedicated to the memory of Fred Graves
(1936–1999)

Silk-Lined Floozies with Tailored Scars

The secret of life is honesty and fair dealing. If you can fake that you've got it made.

Groucho Marx

Not All Monsters Come in Kits

Even Lon Chaney, with wire-
clips, bulged eyeballs, bleeding tongue
and ribboned cheeks, could only
guess at your best agony

and Karloff with his muck-
spreader boots, steel spine and grey
thick grease paint, could only be
kindness, tea and honesty.

Then you came, Rondo Hatton,
no time required in Jack P Pierce's
chair, with his waxed lids, spirit-
gum brows and cotton wool torture.

And the studio had you
cheap, paying for your disease,
your Hyde face untouched by
potion or mythology.

Bathed in lights of the surgery
via Hollywood creeps and monochrome
into nature's callous make-up bag, a
ghoul of doomed integrity.

Beverly Hills, California

*For Rondo Hatton (1894–1946) actor, and sufferer of acromegaly,
which distorted the shape of his head, features and extremities,
making him Hollywood's only ready-made monster.*

Flattery's Not Included

The taproom couple
are permanent fixtures,
beer mat shabby
and dreary damp.
A silent stain
against the peeling walls,
the creeping familiar
of freehouse decay.

Her thinly applied
Saturday lipstick,
animal tested and
twisted dry,
clings to mouth
of line drawn remorse,
cheated of laughter
in bitter lemon,
leathered defence.

His ready-salted,
broken-skin patience
marks a bitter
withdrawal
into last-barrel hope,
a red-eyed search
through smokeless terrain
for exchanges that
they'll

never have.

Gun House

Sarah Lockwood Pardee (1837–1922), who would later become Mrs Sarah Winchester when she married gun magnate William Wirt Winchester, appeared to suffer some sort of nervous breakdown after losing her only daughter, followed by her father and husband some few years later. It is at this point that history is blurred heavily with legend and folklore.

As the story goes, Sarah, racked with grief, approached a medium, seeking solace in his consultation. She received nothing of the sort and instead was informed that she would never find peace until she'd appeased all the souls of the dead killed by her late husband's gun trade.

She promptly relocated west and began building a house, and she went on building that house until she died aged eighty-four. She had intended to build a room for each victim lost to a Winchester rifle; only then would they and she have found rest.

The site of the house (a popular tourist attraction in northern California) is an impressive six acres in total and the house itself is a sprawling and strangely beautiful creation full of lost cellars, stairs that lead to nowhere, dark angled corridors and secret entrances.

Whether Sarah Winchester was insane or, as some have suggested, a charitable benefactor and employer with an amateur's love for architecture, will probably always be unclear. I think it's safe to say that I was obsessed with the former possibility when I wrote this poem.

Those with an interest in this sort of thing might want to dig out a copy of Swamp Thing #45, *a brilliant issue of a superb comic book written (at the time) by the infinitely talented Alan Moore.*

To silhouette promises and curses met
by the Winchester widow mourning bullet-hole debts,
to guests of bone born of lunacy trips,
the muffled torment of morgue-stitched lips,

to empty slabs and absconded plots,
an unholy home where the shadows rot,
to flesh-eaten boys lost to splintering tasks,
corridors lined with skinless masks,

to loyalties warped by cold empty cribs,
carpentry horror and rifle-blown ribs,
to winding stairs creaking with strain,
a burden of whispers and arthritic pain,

to hammered hymns sung for each barrel blast,
to contracts smeared in the blood pooling past,
to a malady creeping in dancehalls unfilled,
to shuffling arms traders and victims re-killed,

to a genocide repeated in rooms that won't end,
to nailed-up damnation in a place of no friends,
to a mortgage of maggots in its crawling expanse,
to the trigger-unhappy, to that black-veiled stance,

to sacrificed doors hung on hinges of guilt,
a penitence birthed
in a house that death built.

Pan Handled

The lost boy moves from town hall steps.
Autumn dead leaves stitched
in cobweb-spun threads
form a mildewed tunic to keep out the night.

He's leaving the company
of rain-mascara'd, waiting girls,
who laugh at the kid with pointy ears
in an effort to block out the cold rejection
of their weather-weary no-show dates.

He'll broker with the bargain bins
and ward off petty Disney crooks,
search in vain for fairy trails,
in a city where the only magic
is spewed across the costume shops,

the flyblown, stained windows
offering cheap, gaudy spells, dressed
in manky leaf-green tights
and stupid feathered
hats for hire.

He'll follow the steps of Barrie's ghost
through gardens lost to retail shadow
up streets of piss-stink doorway homes
and cardboard box economy.

Where skull and crossbone policies
make Poundshop lands of Never Never
to never gain and never reach those
unremembered victory flights.

Where Tinkerbell is Asda fodder,
crocodile commerce more evil than Hook.
Where a cutlass hovers at the throats
in a future rigged by pirate ships.

Alan Moore

be our Northampton,
the anti-dream
magic man, subversive
ancient scream,

spit pages of colour,
dribble maniacs and whores,
tortured supermen
and burning cold wars,

be masked radical,
blow Parliament apart,
watch new wounds bleed
from Whitechapel hearts,

write nine-panel politics
and *Watchmen* blues,
holocaust snogging,
atomic truths,

kiss old ghosts
in the ministry of moths,
a fly-cursed cathedral
for angels and goths,

be lapsed vegetable,
element and beast,
voice of the fire,
wizard and priest,

show us pornography,
cast old spells,

construct new heavens
and give us hell.

Kiss Off

More god of blunder than demon's thunder,
your spandex bursts with flesh at the seams,
a billion dollars' worth of fake blood smiles,
you're a firework fizzled American dream.

You're in the dock as a shock rock cock,
a devil with false teeth and wig,
a geriatric vampire boy,
fat arse stuck in the lighting rig.

On a massive stage, you're a blob of rage,
grease paint smeared over lines cut deep.
Your axe guitar and monster boots
gimmicks that send me straight to sleep.

You're not a bat, you're just a twat,
a fading creature of the night,
strutting tool with his hair on fire,
lipstick-wearing bag of spite.

In the land of mean is the church of Gene,
where the poor must take your sound advice
to get rich quick and blow the lot
on tons of new Kiss merchandise

LE Woman

After the gig.

Midnight, alone on
Long Eaton Station.
Staged reality sets in
and the applause of earlier
peters out, its memory
now a frosty haze
that settles on the
gun-cold tracks.

And a train that
leads to nowhere
is nowhere to be seen.
Whilst the hilltop blink
of distant lights
plays tiggy with
the fog-glimpsed stars.

And he shivers
in the shelter there, a
claustrophobic theatre
of wrappers
and young smokers' gob,
to dream of bed and
cups of tea.

But from the gloom
of platform 1
across the way a shadow
spills,
upon the slabs are
click-clack heels
that form a lonely
film noir scene.

Which turns into
a plumpish girl,
scarf wrapped pale
with fag-burn charm.
A CCTV actress star,
femme fatale with Tesco bag.

Their tired eyes meet
between the sleet;
embarrassed,
both heads dance away
to fix on fished-out
mobile phones,
their courtship
spurned by
handset screens.

Heart-cold realisation
dawns,
a carriage grumbles
through the mist,
on a night that tells
him what he's not
but fails to tell

him what he is.

Pecan Flippers

It's just a turtle,
pecans for flippers,
dark praline, golden sweet,
melting in the café warmth,
its shell a rippled candy truth
seeing the world
through sugared eyes.

She places it before me,
a kiss above the china pot,
lovers' scene framed
in latte steam,
the chit chat
and the tinkled spoons
form an improve romance score.

Outside the town
is what it is, a worried,
sulking, sour face.
An upturned bin of
chaos spilled, across
a lunchtime's bitter rush.

No moments kept in
shiny foil, no brews to
warm the casual heart.
Dragged ghosts haunt the
waking shade of a clock tower's
disapproving glance.

Outside the town is what it is.

Inside we sit,
with our palace of cups.
Chapped hands touch
under tabled hope,
caressing smooth
uncertain years,
melting in the café warmth,
we are a rippled candy truth,
seeing the world
through sugared eyes.

Summery

Dawn sloughs off its
yesterday, slithers over
railing spikes, over grass and
football posts, paper lads and
hammered bikes.

Cars are tin technologies
stabbing at the peaceful green,
which blurs into a swirling
daze, sycamore, sunrise shady scene.

Later in the midday sun,
the sweaty tops off, boys' brigade
march a bothered, shoulder slope
through crowds to find a dark arcade.

Bees attack the Shandy Bass
and soggy sarnie picnic fare,
underneath the oaks that stretch
in mocking, shimmering leafy prayers.

Birds of prey are fluttered specs
flick-book flights of fancy viewed,
V-signs to the street below
in Ken Loach recalled ghosts renewed

till creeping purple bathes the sky
in tattooed lights and penny gaffs,
the day folds in and walks away,

a Lotto card that's now been scratched.

Acknowledgements

Thanks to Clive Birnie, Rob Gee, Melanie Abrahams, Renaissance One, Gabriele Zuccarini, LeftLion, James Walker, Nottingham Writers' Studio, Arts Council England, and Anna Graves for all your help, advice and continued support.